Cesar Chavez

by Kitty Shea

Compass Point Early Biographies

Content Adviser: Lauren Araiza, M.A.,
University of California-Berkeley

Reading Adviser: Susan Kesselring, M.A., Literacy Educator,
Rosemount-Apple Valley-Eagan (Minnesota) School District

COMPASS POINT BOOKS
MINNEAPOLIS, MINNESOTA

Compass Point Books
3109 West 50th Street, #115
Minneapolis, MN 55410

Visit Compass Point Books on the Internet at *www.compasspointbooks.com*
or e-mail your request to *custserv@compasspointbooks.com*

Photographs ©: Hulton/Archive by Getty Images, cover, 4, 19, 24; USDA/ARS/Russell Lee, cover
background; USDA/ARS/Don Schuhart, 6; Victor Aleman, 7; Franklin D. Roosevelt Library, 9;
Joseph Sohm/ChromoSohm Inc./Corbis, 10; Library of Congress, 11; PhotoDisc, 12; Bettmann/Corbis,
13, 16, 18, 25; Michael Rougier/Time Life Pictures/Getty Images, 14, 17; Walter P. Reuther
Library/Wayne State University, 15, 20; Arthur Schatz/Time Life Pictures/Getty Images, 21;
XNR Productions, 22; Ted Streshinsky/Corbis, 23; AP/Wide World Photos/Greg Gibson, 26 (top);
AP/Wide World Photos/Nick Ut, 26 (bottom); HIRB/Index Stock Imagery, 27.

Creative Director: Terri Foley
Managing Editor: Catherine Neitge
Editor: Brenda Haugen
Photo Researcher: Svetlana Zhurkina
Designers/Page production: Bradford Design, Inc./Jaime Martens and The Design Lab
Educational Consultant: Diane Smolinski

Library of Congress Cataloging-in-Publication Data
Shea, Kitty.
Cesar Chavez, leader of migrant farm workers / written by Kitty Shea.
p. cm. — (Compass Point early biographies)
Includes bibliographical references and index.
ISBN 0-7565-0793-6 (hardcover)
1. Chavez, Cesar, 1927—Juvenile literature. 2. Mexican Americans—Biography—Juvenile
literature. 3. United Farm Workers—History—Juvenile literature. 4. Mexican American migrant
agricultural laborers—Biography—Juvenile literature. 5. Migrant agricultural laborers—Labor
unions—United States—History—Juvenile literature. I. Title. II. Series.
HD6509.C48.S54 2005
331.88'13'092—dc22
2004005691

Table of Contents

NOTE: In this book, words that are defined in the glossary are in **bold** *the first time they appear in the text.*

Helping Others Live Better

Cesar Chavez grew up working in the fields of California. He was a migrant farmworker.

Grocery stores are filled with fruits and vegetables. Someone out in a field, orchard, or vineyard had to pick them. Growers often hire migrant workers to care for and **harvest** produce. Migrant workers are people who move from farm to farm to work where help is needed. It's a tough job that pays very little money.

Cesar tried to make the migrant farmworkers' lives better. He showed workers how they could get paid more and be treated better.

This is the story of Cesar Chavez.

People work in a strawberry field.

Tough Times

The Chavez family poses for a photo at Librado's 100th birthday party in 1982. Standing, from left, are Cesar, Ricardo, Vickey, Father Luis Baldomado, Rita, and Librado Jr. Seated are Librado and Juana.

Cesar Chavez knew all about grocery stores. His father, Librado Chavez, ran one when Cesar was a young boy growing up in Arizona. The family also owned a farm.

Cesar was born March 31, 1927. He was named after his grandfather Cesario Chavez. Cesario had moved to the United States from Mexico.

Life was good for Cesar's family. Then came the Great Depression of the 1930s. Many people in the United States lost their jobs during the Depression. Many businesses and banks had to shut down. Most people didn't have any money to spend or save.

Librado had to close his store. For a while, the family lived on what it made on the farm. Then in 1933, a **drought** destroyed the crops. The Chavez family ended up losing the farm, too.

Leaving their farms, many people went to California to look for work.

To make money, Cesar's family moved to California. They worked on farms that belonged to other people.

Living As a Migrant Worker

In the United States, there are between 3 million and 5 million migrant farmworkers.

Workers harvest and box lettuce.

Migrant farmworkers often live in crowded shacks or tents. They may not have electricity or running water. They may not have indoor bathrooms.

Grapes, cherries, lettuce, and other crops grow well in California's valleys. Migrant farmworkers plant, weed, pick, and

This migrant family had to sell their tent shelter ▶ to buy food during the Great Depression.

pack the fruits and vegetables. Then the produce is sent to grocery stores around the country.

Cesar and his family became migrant farmworkers in California. Cesar started working on farms when he was 10. Children had to work when their mothers and fathers

A family of migrant workers harvests grapes in a California vineyard in 1939.

could not make enough money themselves. Sometimes the Chavez family worked all day and only made a dollar.

Cesar's family moved wherever there was work. For years, they didn't have a home.

◄ Grapes growing on a vine

Migrant workers often endured poor living conditions. Old buses were used as homes by some migrant workers in 1959.

When they finally settled in a neighborhood, it was a **slum.**

Working Every Day

Cesar went to school in between farm jobs. He didn't like school. His teachers got angry when he spoke Spanish with his friends.

Cesar quit school after completing the eighth grade to help his family. His father had been injured. Cesar's family now needed him to work every day.

Cesar, 15, holds his diploma after graduating from the eighth grade.

15

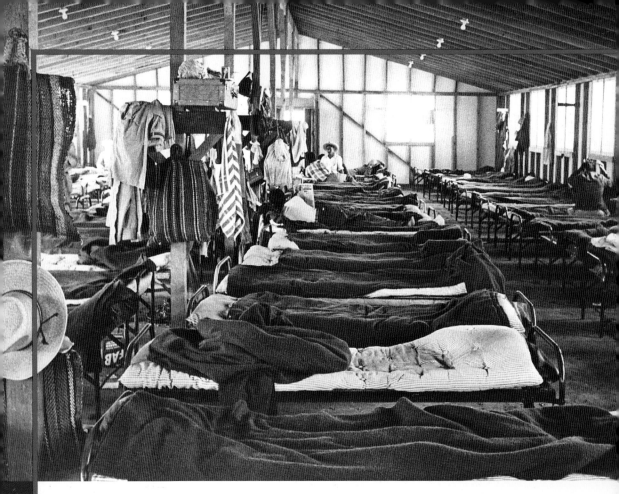

Crowded and dirty, this migrant camp was shut down by the government.

Cesar worked hard for many hours at a time. He still had a hard time paying for food, clothing, and a place to live. He didn't think it was fair he worked so hard to earn so little.

16

Migrant farmworkers take a break to ➤ eat lunch at a California farm in 1959.

Other farmworkers felt the same way. Small groups of them went on **strike.** They refused to work until the growers paid them more.

Usually the growers said no. The growers said they could hire other workers to take their places. Then the unhappy workers would have no jobs.

Cesar (center) talks with Fred Ross as they march to support farmworkers.

Cesar had just about given up on making things better for workers. Then he met Fred Ross. Fred taught poor people how to speak up and fight for their rights in a peaceful way.

Starting a Union

Fred hired Cesar to work for him. Cesar's starting pay was $35 a week. It was more money per week than he had ever made.

Cesar helped Mexican-Americans become United States citizens. He also helped them sign up to vote. Now Cesar was ready to help make life better for migrant farmworkers.

Cesar thought farmworkers should form one big **union.** Then growers would have to listen.

A union political button

The union would try to get the growers to
agree to better wages and working conditions.

Thousands of migrant farmworkers
joined Cesar's union, the National Farm
Workers Association. Their hopes became
the union's cause—or *La Causa,* as Cesar
called it in Spanish.

On Strike

In 1965, Cesar's union went on strike against grape growers. The workers who

Cesar talks with grape pickers in 1968.

picked grapes in California wanted to be paid more. The growers wouldn't raise the workers' pay. What was Cesar going to do?

Cesar needed to get on television and in newspapers to tell people about *La Causa*. Americans needed to know how little money farmworkers made. They needed to know how the farmworkers lived. If they knew, they would

◄ Cesar in front of a *La Causa* poster

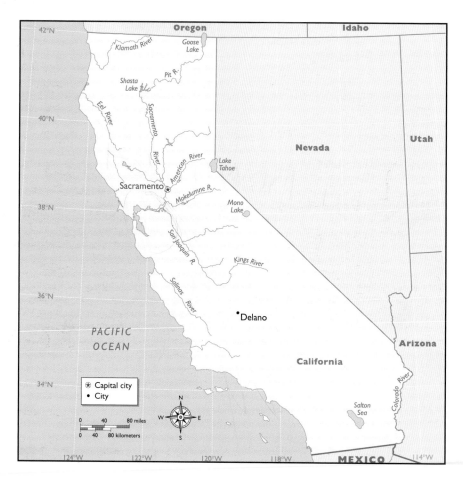

tell the grape growers to treat the grape
pickers better. So Cesar and the grape pickers
walked 340 miles (547 kilometers). They
walked from Delano, California, to Sacramento,

Grape pickers march to Sacramento to protest low wages and poor conditions.

the capital of California. This would get attention.

Cesar also asked Americans to **boycott** grapes. Growers lost lots of money. The grape strike and boycott lasted for five years. In 1970, growers agreed to the union demands. Cesar had helped the farmworkers win.

Standing Up for What Is Right

Later in 1970, Cesar led a strike and boycott against lettuce growers.

He also spoke out against spraying crops with bug killers. Farmworkers were getting sick from the poisonous spray.

More than once, Cesar went on a **hunger strike.** He would stop eating for weeks at a time. This brought attention to the problems of the farmworkers.

Cesar speaks out against the use of pesticides.

Cesar fought for what he felt was right. He never used violence, though. His mother, Juana Chavez, taught him to solve problems by talking. His way took time and patience, but it worked.

◄ Coretta Scott King, the widow of Martin Luther King Jr., marches beside Cesar in New York to support the lettuce boycott.

A Hero for Farmworkers

President Bill Clinton gives Cesar's Presidential Medal of Freedom award to Cesar's widow, Helen Chavez, in 1994.

Cesar was back in Arizona at a farm- worker's home when he died in his sleep on April 23, 1993. He was 66 years old.

Cesar changed the lives of thousands

Cesar E. Chavez Street in Los Angeles

of farmworkers. At his funeral, more than 50,000 people followed his casket. They went past the fields where Cesar had once worked. He was their hero.

Today, all across the United States there are streets, schools, and parks named for Cesar. Others keep doing the work that he started.

◀ The U.S. Postal Service honored Cesar with a stamp in 2003.

Important Dates in Cesar Chavez's Life

1927	Cesar Estrada Chavez born near Yuma, Arizona, on March 31
1937	Family moved to California to become migrant farmworkers
1944	Joined United States Navy and served during World War II
1948	Married Helen Fabela
1962	Started union called the National Farm Workers Association
1965	Union began strike against California grape growers
1966	Marched 340 miles (547 kilometers) from Delano to Sacramento to bring attention to striking farmworkers
1968	Fasted for 25 days to protest the use of violence
1970	Grape strike ended with new contract for grape pickers; started lettuce strike and boycott
1975	California Agricultural Labor Relations Act signed into law to protect farmworkers
1988	Fasted 36 days to protest crop spraying
1993	Died in San Luis, Arizona, at age 66, on April 23
1994	Cesar's widow, Helen Chavez, accepts the Presidential Medal of Freedom in his honor

Glossary

boycott—to refuse to buy something as a form of protest

drought—a long spell of very dry weather

harvest—to pick and gather crops

hunger strike—to stop eating to bring attention to a problem

slum—a crowded, poor, run-down area in a city

strike—when people stop working, hoping to force their employer to agree to things they want

union—an organization of workers

Did You Know?

- Young Cesar attended more than 30 elementary and middle schools. He went to school for a few weeks or months at a time before his family moved on to the next farm.

- Farmworkers are the poorest group of workers in the United States today. Half of all farmworkers earn less than $7,500 per year, which is less than the government's definition of poverty. Cesar never earned more than $6,000 a year.

- Cesar met his wife, Helen, working in California's vineyards. Helen continued to labor as a farmworker after marrying Cesar. They had eight children.

- After Cesar's death, his birthday of March 31 was declared a state holiday in California. In Cesar's honor, his family received the 1994 Presidential Medal of Freedom, the highest award given by the president to civilians.

Want to Know More?

At the Library

Davis, Lucile. *Cesar Chavez: A Photo-Illustrated Biography*. Mankato, Minn.:
  Bridgestone Books, 1998.

Griswold del Castillo, Richard. *Cesar Chavez: The Struggle for Justice*. Houston:
  Piñata Books, 2002.

Krull, Kathleen. *Harvesting Hope: The Story of Cesar Chavez*. San Diego:
  Harcourt Children's Books, 2003.

On the Web

For more information on *Cesar Chavez*, use FactHound
to track down Web sites related to this book.

1. Go to *www.facthound.com*
2. Type in a search word related to this book
   or this book ID: 0756507936.
3. Click on the *Fetch It* button.

Your trusty FactHound will fetch the best Web sites for you!

On the Road

Cesar E. Chavez Education and Retreat Center

29700 Woodford-Tehachapi Road

Old Highway 58

Keene, CA 93531

661/823-6134

To visit the memorial garden and visitors' center around Cesar's gravesite

Index

About the Author

Kitty Shea founded Ideas & Words in 1988 with the goal of following her curiosity into different writing disciplines and subject matter. She has since authored books for young readers, served as editor of home and travel magazines, edited cookbooks, and published hundreds of articles and essays. She has also taught in the journalism department of her alma mater, the University of St. Thomas in St. Paul, Minnesota.